WASHINGTON D.C.

Text by
BRUCE R. SMITH

Photographs by
ANDREA PISTOLESI

BONECHI

Contents

Project and editorial conception: Casa Editrice Bonechi
Publication Manager: Monica Bonechi
Picture research: Monica Bonechi, Mattia Mela.
Graphic design, make-up and editing: Alberto Douglas Scotti, Manuela Ranfagni
Text by Bruce R. Smith

© Copyright by Casa Editrice Bonechi - Florence - Italy - E-mail: bonechi@bonechi.it

Printed in Italy by Centro Stampa Editoriale Bonechi

Photographs from the archives of Casa Editrice Bonechi taken by Andrea Pistolesi,
except page 1 top left © Lester Lefkowitz/The Image Bank/Getty Images, *pages 32 above and 37* © 2004 Getty Images, *page 40 below courtesy of The White
House Historical Association, page 45 middle* © Lee Snider/Photo Images/CORBIS, *page 47 below and page 48 below courtesy of Capsco inc.,
page 50 below* © Fred J. Maroon, *back cover bottom right* © Panoramic Images/Getty Images.

ISBN 88-476-1923-8

www.bonechi.com

INTRODUCTION

International cosmopolis, capital of the United States of America, national center for commerce and the arts, collage of distinctive neighborhoods: Washington, D. C., is all of these places, all at the same time. Riding the city's Metrorail system, you might find yourself sitting next to one of the legislators, lawyers, or lobbyists for which Washington is notorious, but just as easily your fellow passenger might be an economist at the World Bank, or a space scientist, or an authority on African art. Settling in for a performance of the National Symphony at the Kennedy Center, you might overhear the conversation of a diplomat from France, or a specialist in Native American cultures from the Smithsonian, or a student from one of the area's twenty-some colleges and universities. Strolling along the banks of the Potomac River in West Potomac Park, you might spot Capitol Hill staffers tossing a frisbee, workers from the Organization of American States playing soccer, fourth-generation native Washingtonians fishing, families from all over the country enjoying a picnic. When it comes time to eat, there are not only world-class restaurants to choose from but a wide range of smaller places serving the cuisines that have arrived along with new citizens who now call the Washington area home: Afghani, Bolivian, Cambodian, Salvadorian, Ethiopian, Korean, Nicaraguan, Vietnamese. Amid it all, you can find the accents, architectural styles, food, and folkways that make Washington a city of the Piedmont plateau, situated halfway between the Chesapeake Bay to the east and the

Appalachian Mountains to the west. For untold centuries, the land where Washington now stands was hunted, farmed, and fished by Algonquian-speaking Native Americans. Suggestions of the wooded landscape these people knew can be appreciated today in Rock Creek Park. The park runs through the entire length of the northwest part of the city down to the Potomac River, passing by one of the tribes' major soapstone quarries along Piney Branch Parkway. Although Spanish ships explored the Chesapeake Bay in the late sixteenth century, it was not until 1608 that Europeans first arrived in the Potomac valley, when Captain John Smith sailed up the river, possibly as far as the head of navigation at Little Falls, four and a half miles northwest of what is today Arlington Memorial Bridge. Along the way he noted the presence of a Native American settlement called Nacothtank on the present-day site of Anacostia in Southeast Washington. In 1632 Henry Fleete, a fur trader, made the same journey, stopping off at a settlement he called Tohoga, probably near the present-day site of Georgetown. Fleete liked what he saw: "This place is without question the most pleasant and healthful place in all this country and most convenient for habitation, the air being temperate in summer and not violent in winter." Anglo settlement followed these exploratory missions, mostly in huge plantations along both sides of the river. Native people were quickly decimated, in Thomas Jefferson's tactful phrasing, "by smallpox, spiritous liquors, and abridgement of territory." When merchants founded two port cities,

Alexandria in Virginia and Georgetown in Maryland, to handle the shipping and commercial needs of the Potomac plantations, they little dreamed that both places would someday be swallowed up in a huge metropolis. Today Georgetown and Alexandria, two of Washington's most atmospheric neighborhoods, retain dozens of reminders of the colonial past. The event that changed the region forever came in 1790, seven years after the colonies achieved independence from Great Britain, when the Potomac River region was chosen as the site for the capital of the newly formed United States of America. Prophetically enough, it was a political compromise that determined the location, much farther south than anyone from Boston, New York, or Philadelphia would have liked. Two political enemies, Thomas Jefferson and Alexander Hamilton, worked it all out over dinner, managing in the process to resolve—for the time being, at least—an economic stand-off between the northern colonies and the southern that threatened the new republic's very existence. The exact site, at the confluence of the Potomac River with the Anacostia River, was chosen by George Washington. All sorts of people had a hand in making the new city. An African-American mathematician, Benjamin Banneker, joined Andrew Ellicott, a surveyor, in mapping the site. The design itself, a grid bisected by broad avenues that converge on circles and squares, was drawn by Major Pierre Charles L'Enfant, a French engineer who had come to America with the Marquis de Lafayette and had fought in the Revolutionary War.
Washington, as the new seat of government came to be called the first year, was one of the first great cities since Roman times to be planned from the top down. L'Enfant's design was based on principles both aesthetic and practical. "Lines or avenues of direct communication" would serve, in L'Enfant's words, "to connect the separate and most distant objects with the principal, and to preserve through the whole a reciprocity of sight." Such vistas not only produce an imposing effect; they also make it easier to control mobs, as Baron Haussmann realized when he redesigned Paris along similar lines sixty years after Washington was laid out. (Conventional wisdom has it that Washington was inspired by Paris.) The most serious challenge to Washington's development came during the War of 1812, when British troops invaded what General Robert Ross called "this harbor of Yankee democracy" and set fire to the Capitol, the White House, and other public buildings. Afterwards, fully a third of the Congress voted to move the capital somewhere else rather than rebuild. Reconstruction did take place, but as late as 1842 Charles Dickens, surveying vacant lots and rough-and-ready buildings at every turn, could dismiss "the City of Magnificent Distances" as "the City of Magnificent Intentions." Real growth began in the 1850s and has never stopped since. Through it all L'Enfant's plan has been preserved and extended. Original features of the plan like the Capitol and the White House were complemented in the nineteenth century by addition of the Washington Monument, the Old Post Office, and the Smithsonian Castle, at the turn of the twentieth century by the mansions of Dupont Circle and Embassy Row, in the 1930s and

40s by the Federal Triangle, the National Gallery of Art, and the Lincoln and Jefferson Memorials, and in the late twentieth century by the Kennedy Center for the Performing Arts, the Air and Space Museum, the East Building of the National Gallery of Art, the Holocaust Museum, and the Vietnam and Korean war memorials. Scores of new office buildings in downtown Washington and in the West End, all of them at the statutory maximum height established by Congress in 1910, have uniformly raised L'Enfant's grand design into three dimensions. During its two centuries of existence Washington has long since outgrown the ten-mile square envisioned by its founders, spilling over into the adjacent states of Maryland and Virginia. Today the Washington metropolitan area is home to more than four million people in an area that covers 3,957 square miles.

THE MALL

Parade route, rallying ground, outdoor pantheon to America's national heroes, sports field, fairground, seat of the national conscience: the Mall democratically combines all these functions in one of North America's great public spaces. L'Enfant had imagined the Mall as a "place of general resort," to be lined with theaters, assembly halls, academies, and "all sort of places as may be attractive to the learned and afford diversion to the idle." A single grand avenue 400 feet wide, lined with grand houses, was to run down from the Capitol to the site of the Washington Monument, where it would intersect with another broad axis of open space running from the White House down to the Potomac. In 1791, the river's tidal waters lapped at the foot of the monument site. How the Mall came to fulfill L'Enfant's dream is a long, eventful story. During the War of 1812 the future Mall served as a drill ground for British troops. Through the first half of the nineteenth century it remained mostly unlandscaped. The fetid waters of a canal cut the Capitol off from the Mall; tracks of the Baltimore & Pacific Railroad ran across the grounds to a station on the site of the National Gallery of Art. Erection of the Smithsonian Castle in 1855 coincided with a scheme to landscape the Mall along picturesque lines, with groves and meandering paths. The Civil War interrupted those plans: the Mall became a massive military camp. Only at the turn of the twentieth century did L'Enfant's original design get dusted off, when the McMillan Commission, headed by Senator James McMillan of Michigan, drafted the master plan that has gradually been realized over the past hundred years. The Department of Agriculture Building (1905) was the first structure along the Mall to be erected according to the commission's plans, followed a few years later by the National Museum of Natural History (1911). Other museums of the Smithsonian Institution have arisen on sites up and down the Mall: the National Gallery of Art (1941), the National Museum of American History (1964), the National Air and Space Museum (1976). Building of the Lincoln Memorial (1911-22) extended the Mall westward across former bogs and marshes. Today the monumental space of the Mall provides a setting for "learned" and "idle" activities ranging from art appreciation to kite-flying, from protest marches to the annual Boy Scout jamboree.

*The two-mile sweep of **the Mall** constitutes one of the world's most famous urban spaces. Overlooking the prospect is the **U.S. Capitol.***

The Capitol's **west facade** retains the sandstone walls of
the original building, erected between 1800 and 1807. The
dome was raised later, during the Civil War.

THE CAPITOL

Where does the United States of America begin?
Some might say at Philadelphia, on July 4, 1776.
But a good argument could be made that it begins on
an 88-foot rise above the Potomac formerly known as
Jenkins Hill. L'Enfant pronounced the site "a pedestal
waiting for a monument" and chose it for the
centerpiece to his design for the new capital city in
1791. From the Capitol broad avenues radiate in all
directions, just as L'Enfant planned, drawing attention
from all quarters of the city to this central point. It is
here that the central axes of the city cross, dividing
the City of Washington into the four quadrants by
which residents and visitors take their bearings:
Northeast, Southeast, Southwest, Northwest. Literally
as well as figuratively, the avenues converging on the
Capitol draw the nation toward the building in which
the federation's affairs are democratically decided:
Maryland Avenue comes in from the northeast, New
Jersey and Delaware from the north, Pennsylvania
from the northwest. Standing on the Capitol's
expansive west terrace, visitors can look down the
Mall, across the Potomac River, and beyond the hills
of Arlington, Virginia, toward the vast continent that

the new nation eventually came to occupy. In its
present form the Capitol stands as an heroic symbol
of the states' commitment to union. Through the
whole of the Civil War work continued on extensions
to the building that had begun in the 1850s. "If people
see the Capitol going on," Lincoln observed, "... it is
a sign we intend the Union shall go on." The dome
was raised in the depths of the war, reaching
completion on December 2, 1863, when Thomas
Crawford's statue of "Freedom" was lifted into place
amid volleys of ceremonial gun fire from the twelve
forts that encircled the beleaguered city.
The Capitol as it stands today still presents the
simple three-part arrangement envisioned by
William Thornton, the physician and amateur
architect who won the competition for the building's
design in 1793. Facing the east facade, with the
Supreme Court and the Library of Congress behind
them, visitors can distinguish three clear units: a
pavilion for the Senate on the right, a pavilion for the
House of Representatives on the left, and a central
rotunda. Though the idea of three components has
remained the same, the structure of the building has

The Capitol's **west facade** (left) retains the sandstone walls of the original building, erected between 1800 and 1807.

The **west terraces** of the Capitol (above) were laid out by Frederick Law Olmsted, designer of New York's Central Park.

passed through four phases of development.

The **first phase** saw the realization of Thornton's basic design, with help from Benjamin Henry Latrobe, the first American-born professional architect. The cornerstone was set in place on November 18, 1793, by George Washington. First a pavilion for the Senate (1800) and then one for the House (1807) were completed, linked by a covered wooden walkway in place of Thornton's unbuilt rotunda. The Senate and the House pavilions, each with its own small dome, are visible today to the right and the left of the central portico. Nineteenth-century extensions have turned them into links in a much larger design. It was Thornton and Latrobe's building that British soldiers put to the torch in 1814, using books from the Library of Congress as kindling.

After the war work began on the **second phase** of the Capitol's construction, a restoration of Thornton and Latrobe's House and Senate pavilions, with the addition of a central rotunda that featured a large, 55-foot-high dome, designed by Charles Bulfinch along the lines of the dome he had supplied for the Massachusetts Statehouse in Boston.

In the **third phase** of construction the Capitol assumed its present form. The need for more space in the 1850s prompted Congress to commission some extensions. Thomas U. Walter designed the wings for the House (completed 1857) and the Senate (1859) that are still in use today. Walter's new construction more than doubled the building's length—from 352 feet to 746 feet—making Bulfinch's dome seem much too small. A new dome, the one that still crowns the edifice, rose to take the place of Bulfinch's dome in 1863. One of the great engineering feats of the nineteenth century, the nine-million-pound dome is made up of two cast-iron shells, one set inside the other. Painted outside and in to resemble marble, the cast-iron structure is not only stronger than stone but lighter and more flexible. The ultimate inspiration for Walter's design was Michelangelo's dome for St. Peter's in Rome (1546-90), but more immediately the cast-iron dome of St. Isaac's Cathedral in St. Petersburg (1842).

In the **fourth and final phase** of construction (1959-60) the central pavilion's eastern front was brought forward 32 feet 6 inches, a refinement Walter had proposed a century earlier.

The Capitol's interior spaces, all of them sumptuously decorated, are dominated by the Great Rotunda, 95 feet 8 inches in diameter and 183 feet high. Under canopy of the dome is a 6000-square-foot fresco of "The Apotheosis of Washington,"

*The cast-iron **dome** of the U.S. Capitol is one of the great engineering feats of the nineteenth century. It is topped by Thomas Crawford's 19-foot **statue of Freedom.***

*Costantino Brumidi's fresco **The Apotheosis of Washington** crowns the dome's interior (left); the **Old Senate Chamber** (bottom left) is a feature of the original building.*

showing the first president attended by figures embodying Liberty and Victory and the Thirteen Original States, along with War, Agriculture, Mechanics, Commerce, Maritime Operations, and the Arts and Sciences. The artist, Costantino Brumidi (1805-1880), had worked in the Vatican before emigrating to America.

North of the Great Rotunda, the Old Senate Chamber was the site of legendary speeches by John C. Calhoun, Henry Clay, and Daniel Webster. The Supreme Court sat in this room from 1860 until it moved across the street in 1935. In the small rotunda just outside can be seen one of the Capitol's most charming features, columns designed by Latrobe that substitute indigenous American plants—maize, tobacco, and cotton—for the acanthus leaves of classical Corinthian columns. Beyond lies the new Senate Chamber. South of the Rotunda, enroute to the new House of Representatives Chamber, is to be found the lower house's old chamber, which has served since 1864 as Statuary Hall. A bronze star on the floor marks the spot where former President John Quincy Adams collapsed during a fatal stroke in 1848.

*The pompous **exterior** of the Library of Congress has had its critics, but the building's sumptuous **interior** dazzles most visitors.*

LIBRARY OF CONGRESS

A rugged granite exterior, looking more than a little like Charles Garnier's Paris Opera House, contains some of Washington's most sumptuous interiors. Created by an act of Congress in 1800, the library started out as a reference collection strictly for the use of senators and congressmen, but by the time it moved into its present main quarters in 1897 it had become, in effect, the American equivalent of the British Library or the Bibliothèque Nationale. The interior proclaims the institution's command over the empire of learning. In the main entrance hall, a huge stained-glass skylight illuminates the richly colored mosaics that cover the vaults of the ceilings and the expanse of the floors.

Computer terminals have replaced the concentric card catalogue cases of the original design—a technological necessity in a library that now contains more than 75 million items on 350 miles of bookshelves. The library occupies not only the landmark Jefferson Building but two adjacent structures: the Art-Deco Adams Building (1939) and the post-modern Madison Building (1980).

SUPREME COURT

Headquarters of the judicial branch of the federal government, as the Capitol is headquarters of the legislative branch and the White House of the executive branch, the Supreme Court occupies a gleaming white marble building just across from the east front of the Capitol. With its magnificent Corinthian columns, the building resembles a Roman temple—but a temple with a thoroughly modern, thoroughly American dedication to "Equal Justice Under Law," as an inscription over the porch proclaims. On the pediment above, sculpted icons of Liberty, Order, and Authority are flanked by likenesses of several real-life personages standing in for Council and Research. Among them are William Howard Taft, the only man to serve both as President of the United States and as Chief Justice of the Supreme Court, and Cass Gilbert, the building's architect. Large sculpted figures by James Earle Fraser on each side of the steps portray, on the left, Contemplation of Justice and, on the right, Authority of Law. After occupying various temporary sites, including the Old Senate Chamber of the Capitol, the court moved into its own building in 1935.

Ancient Roman design principles and American idealism meet in the **Supreme Court's entrance portico.**

The Baths of Diocletian in Rome inspired the station's **vaulted interior.**

Lorado Taft's **Columbus Memorial Fountain** *(1908) dominates Union Station's entrance plaza.*

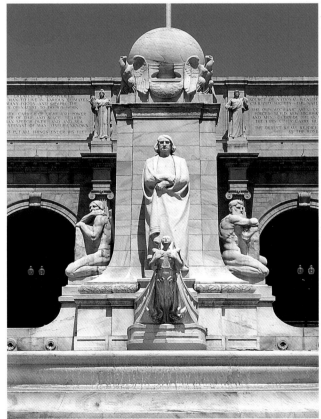

UNION STATION

Monument to memorable events in history, hub of transportation, shopping mall, entertainment complex: the newly refurbished Union Station magnificently combines all these functions. The architect was Daniel H. Burnham, director of works for the 1893 Columbian Exhibition in Chicago. Christopher Columbus, whose 1492 voyage inspired the Chicago exhibition, presides over Union Station's entrance plaza in a monumental fountain designed by Lorado Taft. After passing through the triumphal arches of the portico, visitors arrive in one of Washington's great public spaces. A gigantic barrel vault, deeply coffered and tricked out with gold leaf, sweeps over the two million cubic feet of the former main waiting room. The former first-class waiting room now houses shops, while the former Presidential Suite, originally designed for the president's private use and for receiving important visitors, has been turned into an elegant restaurant.

*Design principles of the **Pantheon** in Rome have been realized in pink marble from Tennessee.*

NATIONAL GALLERY OF ART

Youngest among the world's great museums of western art, the National Gallery owes its existence to the vision, the personal collection, and the money of a private citizen, Andrew W. Mellon (1855-1937). As early as 1841 the federal government, not by design or intent, had fallen heir to a small, miscellaneous collection of paintings that were organized as the National Institute and installed in the Patent Office building. The collection still existed in Mellon's day—it shared quarters with dinosaur bones, prodigious gems, and Native American pots in the Museum of Natural History—but Mellon had something grander in mind: a gallery of European masterpieces to rival the National Gallery of London, the Louvre, the Uffizi, the

Kunsthistorisches Museum, and the Prado, in a building that would bear comparison with its European counterparts. The National Gallery of Art is the realization of Mellon's vision. Opened in 1941, the gallery's West Building joins the Jefferson Memorial (1943) as the city's last great edifices in the idiom of neo-classicism. Both were designed by John Russell Pope. On the exterior, five shades of pink marble from a quarry in Tennessee are subtly modulated from the darkest shade at ground level to the lightest on the dome. The central rotunda, modeled on the Pantheon in Rome, pivots on the light and airy figure of Mercury by the sixteenth-century Flemish-Italian master Giovanni Bologna. From the rotunda, grand corridors lead off east and west to almost a hundred galleries.

Mellon, whose family wealth came from banking and coal, coke, and iron production, had bought his first painting at the age of 27 while touring the great art capitals of Europe with another young Pittsburgh millionaire, Henry Clay Frick. Old Master paintings of the eighteenth century and earlier were the focus of Mellon's interest. By the time he donated his accumulated treasures to the nation and had built a gallery to receive them, the collection included 126 paintings and 26 pieces of sculpture—the largest such gift ever made by a single individual to a governmental entity. His most publicized acquisitions had come in 1931, when Josef Stalin sold off pictures from the collection that Catherine the Great had amassed in the Hermitage Palace in St. Petersburg. Three of the National Gallery's most celebrated holdings—Botticelli's "Adoration of the Magi" and Raphael's "St. George and the Dragon" and "The Virgin Mary with the Christ Child and St. John"— entered the collection at that time. The third, called the Alba Madonna after the Duke of Alba, an earlier owner, has the distinction of being the first painting for which a collector was willing to pay more than a million dollars. When Mellon first notified President Roosevelt of his intention to create a national museum, he expressed his hope that the bequest would "attract gifts from other citizens who may in the future desire to contribute works of art ... to form a great national collection." Almost immediately his gesture had just that effect. The Kress Collection of Italian art, including many pre-Renaissance panels, was installed along with Mellon's pictures and sculptures when the National Gallery opened in

*The generosity of private citizens, not the wealth of a royal dynasty, has produced **one of the world's most important collections of European and American art.***

*Pictures from the Samuel H. Kress Collection, including "Mary Queen of Heaven" by the Dutch Master of the St. Lucy Legend (bottom right, in the center), form the core of the gallery's **collection of medieval and early Renaissance art.***

*Highlights of the National Gallery's collection include "A Girl with a Watering Can" (1876) by **Auguste Renoir**, "Woman with a Parasol-Madame Monet with Her Son" (1875) by **Claude Monet**, and "La Mousmé" (1888) by **Vincent van Gogh** (left). The National Gallery owes its existence to the vision, the personal collection and the money of a private citizen, Andrew W. Mellon (1855-1937).*

1941. Major bequests have since come from Joseph Widener, whose Rembrandts, Vermeers, and El Grecos are among the National Gallery's prizes; from Chester Dale, who contributed major pictures by Monet, Cézanne, Gauguin, Degas, Renoir, Mary Cassatt, George Bellows, and Picasso; from Lessing J. Rosenwald, who provided the prints and drawings department with its core collection; and from scores of other private collectors, including Andrew Mellon's daughter Ailsa Mellon Bruce and his son Paul Mellon. Later acquistions have continued to fulfill the original vision of a museum centered on Old Masters—the only picture by Leonardo da Vinci in the western hemisphere, a portrait of Ginevra de Benci, entered the collection in 1967— but the collection's range has expanded to include nineteenth- and twentieth-century art, as well as work by living artists. Special exhibitions are among the major cultural events in Washington each season.

*I. M. Pei's design for the National Gallery's **East Building** incorporates **glass pyramids** similar to those he later installed in the courtyard of the Louvre.*

NATIONAL GALLERY OF ART
EAST BUILDING

When the National Gallery of Art opened in 1941 there were, by one person's calculations, 24 works of art to the acre. Whole galleries stood empty. Bequests over the years and an expansion of the gallery's scope to include twentieth-century art resulted, by the 1960s, in an overcrowded building. Andrew Mellon, having foreseen such a need, had reserved a site for expansion as part of the deed donating the original gallery to the nation. The unusual shape of the site (Pennsylvania Avenue's intersection with the other streets forms a trapezoid), its conspicuous location where the Mall meets Capitol Hill, and the neoclassical conservatism of John Russell Pope's original building all presented challenges to the commissioned architect, I. M. Pei. The architect's solution was brilliantly simple: Pei divided the trapezoid into two overlapping triangles, designating one triangle for gallery space and the other for offices, support facilities, and the gallery's large reference library. The new building opened in 1978. Triangles supply the basic unit in Pei's design. The plaza between the original gallery (the West Building) and the new structure (the East Building) covers an underground connection illuminated by pyramid-shaped skylights anticipating those that Pei later installed in the courtyard of the Louvre. Polygonal towers anchor the building to the site. Huge planes of pink marble (from the same quarry that supplied the West Building) meet at acute angles. As the viewer walks around, the

Sculptural works *commissioned for the East Building include "Orniforme" (1977) after a design by Jean Arp.*

planes seem to shift and move in relationship to each other. At the apex of one of the triangles, to the right of the entrance, the angle where the planes meet is so acute (just 19 degrees) that one of them seems to be as thin as a sheet of paper—a sheet of paper, that is to say, 107 feet high. What the viewer confronts is, in effect, a huge piece of sculpture.

Inside the East Building triangles dictate the shape of the atrium. Even the skylights are defined as concave pyramids. Pei himself has suggested that the source of the building's excitement is the fact that every area, inside and out, possesses not two but three axes, not two but three vanishing points. The result, for most visitors, is a sensation of lively movement. The effect is enhanced by a blue and orange 86-foot-long mobile, slowly turning in the atrium's airy openness, which was commissioned from Alexander Calder specifically for this space. A tapestry by Joan Miró, also commissioned as a permanent feature, provides a rich textural contrast to the smoothness of the pink marble walls and floors. Galleries of varied shapes and sizes open off the atrium. The East Building houses most of the National Gallery's collection of modernist and contemporary art, but earlier pictures are also on display. An annual series of special exhibitions fills galleries that were designed just for that purpose. The combination of a varied and changing collection, exhibited in one of the most exciting architectural spaces in the world, makes the East Building one of the most visited museums in America.

*The **triangular spaces** (above, left) of the East Building's interior provide a dynamic setting for numerous stationary objects, including (centre) **Jean Dubuffet's "Site à l'Homme Assis"** (1969-84). **George Segal's "The Dancers"** (1982) simulate a turn on the floor (below).*

NATIONAL ARCHIVES

The original copies of the Declaration of Independence (1776), the Constitution of the United States of America (1787), and the Bill of Rights (1791) are the primary reason that millions of visitors pass each year through the doors of the gigantic mausoleum that John Russell Pope raised in 1935 to house the letters, maps, official documents, diaries, photographs, newspapers, ships' logs, motion pictures, sheet music, microfilms, tape recordings, and assorted emphera produced by the United States government and many of its citizens over the course of two centuries.

The Archives' three great treasures are displayed in a monumentally large room, inside cases of protective glass, sealed with inert helium. Every night automatic devices lower the documents into a bombproof vault. It was not until 1952 that the three foundation documents of the American nation were finally united under one roof.

More personal reasons draw other visitors to the National Archives. Census records dating back to 1790, military service records, and ship-passenger arrival lists allow amateur genealogists to trace their family history.

The building's interior displays original copies of the foundational documents of the American political system, including the **Constitution.**

A **sculpted figure of Guardianship** *by James Earle Fraser keeps watch over the Constitution Avenue entrance to the National Archives.*

Erected in 1911, the **Museum of Natural History** was one of the first buildings in the twentieth-century scheme to realize L'Enfant's original plan for the Mall.

NATIONAL MUSEUM OF NATURAL HISTORY
NATIONAL MUSEUM OF MAN

The museum's collection runs to 121 million items. The largest African bush elephant ever shot, all eight tons of it, greets visitors as they arrive in the museum's 125-foot-high rotunda. Corridors on three floors lead off into the various domains of learning. Preserved specimens of animals still inhabiting the world today are exhibited in naturalistic settings. North American species like moose, caribou, mountain goats, grizzly bears, and pumas in one area yield place to African animals in another, African animals to Asian animals in a third. Birds of every climate perch and stare. Visitors are given a rare opportunity to observe penguins close up. Among the fish in the museum's collection is a model of a 92-foot blue whale. To guide them in mounting the preserved specimens, Smithsonian taxidermists began in the 1880s to keep living specimens of some species in pens and cages behind the Castle building. The Smithsonian animals proved so popular with visitors that the zoo was made permanent. In 1889 the live-animal collection—including six bison that had grazed on the Mall—moved to a 163-acre site in Rock Creek Park and became the National Zoo. "Amazonia," a rainforest habitat that is home to free-ranging species, is indicative of the zoo's new self-definition as a BioPark that stresses the natural interdependence of all forms of life. The geology galleries of the Natural History

Museum are crammed with stalactites and stalagmites from famous American caverns, every imaginable kind of mineral from around the world, and meteorites from Outer Space. For most visitors, however, the "stars" of the geological collection are the gems. Huge finished stones like a 138-carat ruby, a 157-carat emerald, a 234-carat topaz, and a 330-carat star sapphire serve as foils for the Hope Diamond, which at 49.5 carats ranks as the largest blue diamond in the world. The third great collecting area, anthropology, has recently become a museum in its own right. Visitors can study skeletal remains and cultural artefacts from all over the globe, including a hand axe from Kenya that is 700,000 years old. Murals and dioramas create a visual context for inserting these objects into the natural environments and social contexts in which they were produced and used. The museum's collection of artefacts is particularly strong on the indigenous peoples of North and South America. Changing special exhibitions focus on particular cultures and assemble artefacts from specialist museums in other parts of the world. At the annual Folklife Festival on the Mall, the Smithsonian brings to Washington representatives of one or more of America's many cultures and ethnic traditions. For a week each July these people tell stories, sing, dance, cook, and practice traditional crafts.

THE FOSSILS

The imperial feeling of the building housing the National Museum of Natural History (completed 1911) is altogether appropriate for a collection that asserts authority over three realms of knowledge — anthropology, biology, and geology — and brings together specimens from all over the world.

From the central rotunda corridors lead off into the three domains of knowledge.

On the biological front, the museum displays the remains of plants and animals that predate man.

They range in size from insects preserved in amber to the bones of Diplodocus, a sauropod dinosaur measuring more than 80 feet from head to tail.

Among the fossils on display the oldest is a cabbage-size mass formed by micro-organisms 3.5 billion years ago.

Life-like displays in the Museum of Natural History turn scientific knowledge into things that visitors can see, hear, and in some cases touch.

The museum's **collection of fossils** extends back to the beginnings of life in the sea 3.5 billions years ago.

The Smithsonian started out as an institute for the study of natural history, conventional enough in the mid-nineteenth century, but in short order it began to accumulate the miscellaneous items that have earned it a description as "the nation's attic." First came the model collection from the U. S. Patent Office. Then Congress deposited all the left-over exhibits from the Philadelphia Centennial Exposition of 1876. The Smithsonian has gone on collecting and never looked back. Assembled under one roof in the Museum of American History (opened 1964) are George Washington's false teeth, Judy Garland's ruby slippers from "The Wizard of Oz," Edison's original light bulb, the largest lump of anthracite coal ever excavated, Henry Ford's Model T, thousands of everyday household objects dating back to colonial times, an authentic stagecoach, linotype machines, gunboats from the eighteenth century, some of the earliest computers—and a seated statue of a toga-clad George Washington (by Horatio Greenough, 1840) that there was nowhere else to put. All over the museum reconstructed room settings provide a context for the thousands of objects on display. In some of these settings—an authentic country post office, for example—visitors can actually walk in and participate. In the case of a 1910 drug store, they can even order a soda.

Items in "the nation's attic" include a statue of
Washington in Roman costume *that graced the Capitol rotunda until it cracked the floor.* **Boats and ships** *are among transportation exhibits together with antique automobiles, steam locomotives, and a railroad passenger coach dating to 1836.*

*The Botanic Garden's aluminum and glass conservatories provide ideal environments for plants from all over the world, including a renowned **cactus collection**.*

UNITED STATES BOTANIC GARDEN

The stone front of the U. S. Botanic Garden, pretending to be the *orangerie* of a seventeenth-century French chateau, ushers visitors into a gigantic greenhouse made of aluminum and glass. At the time it was built in 1931 it was the largest such structure in the world. Precise climate controls make it possible to provide ideal conditions for plants from all over the globe. Inside the building flourish collections of orchids, begonias, cacti, palms, bromeliads, epiphytes, carnivors, and cycads. Survivors from the age of dinosaurs, cycads produce seeds the size of hen's eggs. Twelve thousand orchids and 313 different types of cactus rank these particular collections among the largest in the world. Several political leaders of the early republic, among them Washington, Jefferson, and Madison, supported the idea of a national botanic garden. The first conservatory was constructed in 1842 to house exotic specimens that explorers brought back from the South Seas. Offspring of some of the original plants are still in the collection. Since 1849 the garden has been located at the eastern end of the Mall. The site it occupies today stands between two beautifully designed natural sites. Eastward stretch the slopes of Capitol Hill, as landscaped in the 1870s by Frederick Law Olmsted, the designer of Central Park in New York City. The west terrace of the Capitol, with its parterres and grand stairways, is Olmsted's creation, as are the monumental lampstands that surround the Capitol grounds. South of the Botanic Garden's greenhouses are geometrically laid out flower beds that provide the setting for a spectacular fountain executed by Frédéric Auguste Bartholdi, designer of the Statue of Liberty, for the 1876 Centennial Exhibition in Philadelphia. Three nymphs in bronze hold up a large basin rimmed with lamps. Electric lights have replaced the gas jets that made the fountain one of the first self-illuminated urban monuments in the world. In addition to Bartholdi Park, the Botanic Garden maintains just west of the conservatory a three-acre demonstration garden in which vegetables and other useful plants are grown each season.

*Earlier periods in aviation history are represented by aircraft that includes (above) the original **Wright brothers' "Flyer."***

***Rockets from America's space exploration program** are gathered in the missile pit of Space Hall, along with the **Hubble Space Telescope** (left).*

NATIONAL AIR AND SPACE MUSEUM

Drawing more than ten million visitors a year, the National Air and Space Museum has plausible claims to being the most visited museum in the world. American achievement in flight is the focus of the museum's displays—the building itself opened on July 4, 1976, the two hundredth anniversary of the Declaration of Independence—but the dream of defying mankind's earth-boundedness clearly has an appeal that goes beyond national borders. Twenty-three galleries, covering 200,000 square feet, organize the vast spaces of the building's interior. Gathered in the main hall are planes, rockets, and spacecraft that mark important "Milestones of Flight." Most are originals, not models or copies. The dateline leads from the Wright brothers' "Flyer," which stayed airborne for 59 seconds at Kitty Hawk, North Carolina, in 1903, to the command module "Columbia" that carried astronauts Neil Armstrong, Buzz Aldrin, and Michael Collins to the moon and back in 1969. Highlights along the way include "The Spirit of St. Louis," in which Charles Lindbergh became the first individual to fly nonstop across the Atlantic (1927); the Bell X-1, the first plane to fly beyond the speed of sound (1947); the back-up vehicle for Explorer 1, the first successful American sattelite (1958); "Friendship 7," the Mercury spacecraft in which John Glenn became the first American to orbit the earth (1962); the Gemini IV EVA that carried Edward H. White II for the first U.S. walk in space (1965); and the prototype of Pioneer 10, the first spacecraft to explore the outer planets of the solar system. Smaller than any of these exhibits in size but just as large in fascination is a piece of rock from the moon, collected by Apollo 17. Visitors are invited to reach out and touch it. Galleries leading off from the entrance hall explore various aspects of flight. Interactive exhibits on "How Things Fly" start with the basics. The boost given to flight technology by both world wars is apparent in the museum's large collection of vintage aircraft. A gallery called "Where Next, Columbus?" presents some of the challenges that space exploration continues to pose. Two facilities make the solar system and the experience of flight breath-takingly immediate: the Albert Einstein Planetarium, equipped with a Zeiss Model VI projector, and the Samuel P. Langley Theater, where films on flight and the environment are projected.

*Vintage of **commercial aircraft** and **fighter planes** trace the history of flight in the twentieth century*

MOONWALK

Spacecraft on display at the National Air and Space museum include the Apollo lunar module, the backup to the first lunar module flown in orbit.

HIRSHHORN MUSEUM

Art-in-the-round arrived on the Mall in 1974 in the form of the Joseph H. Hirshhorn Museum and Sculpture Garden. Gordon Bunshaft's idiosyncratic building instantly provoked controversy but the art collection that it contains just as quickly established itself as a fixture in Washington's cultural life. Arriving in America from a Latvian ghetto at the age of six, Joseph Hirshhorn was a millionaire several times over by the age of 28. All of his passion and a great deal of his money went into amassing what may be the largest art collection ever assembled by a private individual: 4000 paintings and 2000 pieces of sculpture. In the years just after World War II, when New York was the center of the world market in contemporary art, Hirshhorn was buying on a scale approached by no one else. The result is an accumulation of modern art that has both breadth and depth—two qualities that also distinguish the concrete cylinder that contains the collection. The museum is the site of frequent special exhibitions and an acclaimed film series.

Henry Moore's "Two-Piece Reclining Figure: Points" (1969-70) *frames the Hirshhorn Museum's defiantly un-classical frontage on the Mall (below).* **Circular galleries** *give visitors a distinctive perspective on twentieth-century art. Another particularly striking focal point is (left)* **Henry Moore's "Falling Warrior"** *(1956-57).*

HIRSHHORN SCULPTURE GARDEN
AND OTHER SMITHSONIAN ART MUSEUMS

In a city where statues typically stand atop pedestals and pediments the Hirshhorn Museum's sculpture garden brings statuary down to a human level. More than 300,000 people each year are enticed to descend from the Mall into a sunken garden laid out with trees, grassy lawns, shrubs, and several dozen pieces of modern sculpture. The garden's two levels invite wandering, small spaces facilitate close-up observation, benches encourage lingering. In date the pieces on display range from the late nineteenth century, when modernism first emerged as a distinct style, to the 1950s and 60s, when Joseph Hirshhorn was most active as a collector. The 1.3-acre Sculpture Garden shows only a part of the museum's huge collection of three-dimensional art. On the plaza beneath the elevated mass of the museum building—itself a piece of sculpture—are Claes Oldenburg's ''Geometric Mouse'' and Tony Cragg's witty ''Subcommittee.'' Circular galleries inside the museum contain major pieces by Degas, Picasso, and Giacometti, as well as mixed-media installations.

Several other specialist art museums are also part of the Smithsonian Institution. The Freer Gallery displays an unusual collection of Asian art and turn-of-the-century American art assembled by Detroit industrialist Charles Lang Freer (1854-1919). The gallery's collection of works by James McNeill Whistler (1834-1903) ranks as the largest and most important in the world.

The Sackler Gallery, founded in 1987 with a group of one thousand Asian masterpieces collected by Arthur M. Sackler, M.D., is not restricted, as the Freer is, to showing only its own holdings. Temporary exhibitions of objects from other Asian art museums and shows of work by living artists make the Sackler a lively center for the study of Asian culture across many centuries and geographic areas. The cultural traditions of the 25 million Americans who trace their ancestry to sub-Saharan Africa find visual expression in the array of objects on display in the Museum of African Art. The permanent collection includes not only the ceremonial masks and figures for which Africa is best known in Europe and America but utilitarian objects that integrate art with everyday life in Africa itself.

Sharing space with grass, trees, and sky in the **Hirshhorn Sculpture Garden** *are (clockwise from top right) Giacomo Manzu's ''Young Girl on a Chair'' (1955), Jean Ipousteguy's ''Man Pushing Door'' (1966) and Marino Marini's ''Horse and Rider'' (1952-53).*

*In the nineteenth century the picturesque towers of the **Smithsonian Castle building** formed the centerpiece of a Romantic landscape that included groves of trees, wandering paths, and a small herd of bison.*

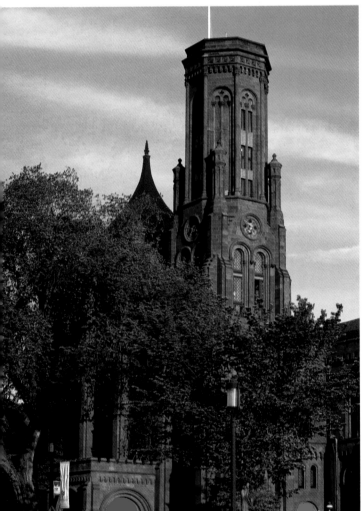

SMITHSONIAN CASTLE

The museums and research institutes that line the Mall—a complex that forms, in effect, America's "National Museum"—owe their existence to someone who never laid foot on American soil in his lifetime. When James Smithson, illegitimate son of the first Duke of Northumberland, died in 1829, he willed his entire estate of £ 104,000 in the first instance to his nephew and, failing an heir, to the United States government "to found at Washington, under the name of the Smithsonian Insitution, an establishment for the increase and diffusion of knowledge among men." Six years later Smithson's nephew died, heirless. It took Congress an astonishing nine years to decide to accept Smithson's bequest, but the result was a research institution devoted primarily to natural history and housed in the red Neo-Gothic prodigy now popularly known as "the Smithsonian Castle." An irregular array of towers and turrets, James Renwick's 1855 structure fitted in perfectly with the meandering paths and picturesque groves that characterized the Mall in the mid nineteenth century. Disinterred from its original resting place in Scotland, Smithson's body shares space today with the administration of the institution his money founded.

Classic marble and monumental bronze take on the **brutal shapes of the concentration camps** *in which millions perished under Nazi rule.*

Artistic responses to the Holocaust *by American schoolchildren (right) line one of the museum's corridors;* **visual documents of camp horrors** *(below right) provide a context for hundreds of personal objects left behind by inmates.*

U.S. HOLOCAUST MEMORIAL MUSEUM

In a city full of monuments, the U. S. Holocaust Memorial Museum provokes particularly strong and immediate reactions from visitors. Since its opening in 1993, it has quickly established itself as a major destination. Standing within the shadow of the Washington Monument and commanding a view of the Tidal Basin, the building displays an uneasy relationship with its celebratory environment. On the outside the Holocaust Museum makes superficial gestures of compatibility with its neighborhoods, the red-brick Auditors' Building and the Bureau of Printing and Engraving, but on the inside visitors are confronted at once with the brutal, factory-like functionality that characterized the Nazi-run death camps in which millions of Jews, political dissidents, homosexuals, and others were murdered during the 1930s and 40s. Contrast between the structure's brutality and its human content is striking: on display are clothing, shoes, photographs, personal mementos, and diaries that belonged to individual inmates, along with one of the actual railway cars used to transport Polish Jews to Treblinka.

*Ten times taller than its classical exemplars, the Washington Monument stands as **the tallest masonry structure in the world**.*

WASHINGTON MONUMENT

The cenotaph honoring America's Revolutionary War general and first president remains the tallest masonry structure in the world. At the time it was completed in 1884 it was, indeed, the tallest structure of any kind in the world. At 555 feet 5 inches the Washington Monument is nearly twice as high as the U. S. Capitol, five times higher than any other building in Washington—and ten times higher than any of the Egyptian obelisks that provided models for its design. That such an elegantly simple structure should have such a complicated political history is one of the great ironies of Washington. As early as 1783 the Continental Congress voted to erect a statue of George Washington on horseback wherever the permanent capital came to be. L'Enfant duly provided a location just where the east-west axis from the Capitol crosses the north-south axis

from the president's house. When Jefferson tried to place a small marker on the precise spot, the ground proved too boggy to support anything. It was therefore at a higher, drier location 350 feet northeast of L'Enfant's intended spot that work actually began on the monument on July 4, 1848. A private society, founded fifteen years earlier, provided enough funds to get started and a grandiose plan by Robert Mills, who had designed the monumental column that honors Washington's memory in Baltimore. Difficulties lay ahead. Money problems led to the scrapping of the circular mausoleum Mills had envisioned around the base. Political vandalism (xenophobic "Know-Nothings" first stole an ancient Roman block of stone contributed by Pope Pius IX and then took over the society itself) brought construction to a halt at 156 feet. Then came the Civil War. Cattle for feeding the troops grazed around the base of what Mark Twain called "a factory chimney with the top broken off." When work resumed in 1876 with Congressional support, Mills' design was altered yet again, this time insuring that the finished structure would observe the classical proportions of a height ten times the size of the base. The result is a perfect replica of an ancient obelisk, albeit in a world where people are 60 feet tall. On the inside high-speed elevators and 898 steps take visitors past commemorative stones contributed by numerous foreign countries, many of the states, and a very odd assortment of private societies.

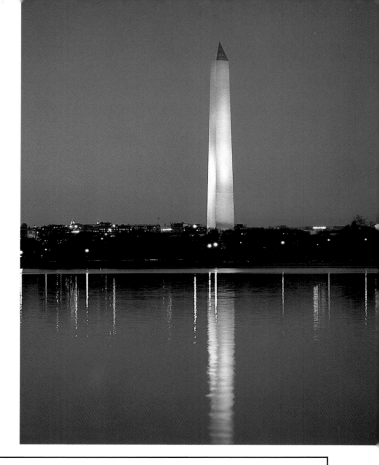

*At different times of day and night, the **distinctive silhouette of the Washington Monument** turns varying faces of white, gray, gold, and pink to the surrounding city.*

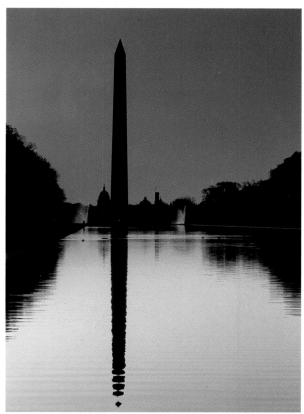

REFLECTING POOL

Stretching nearly 2000 feet from the base of the Lincoln Memorial to the foot of the Washington Monument, the Reflecting Pool helps define one of Washington's grandest vistas. Two miles in the distance looms the dome of the Capitol. In the middle distance rises the magnificent thrust of the Washington Monument. On clear days, visitors to the Lincoln Memorial can look eastward and see the marble mass of the Washington Monument reflected as a shimmering image, disturbed from time to time by swimming ducks and splashing children. Tree-lined avenues down both sides of the pool invite strollers to linger, while jets of water at the Pool's eastern end catch the sunlight and turn it into rainbows. By night, the pool reflects the lighted monument amid the moon and stars. As the pool was nearing completion in the early 1920s, architect Henry Bacon and his friends celebrated by staging a moonlight regatta of flower-trimmed boats. More recent years have seen the launching of a flotilla of hundreds of candles to mark the memory of victims of AIDS.

*Open to the changing sky, the **Reflecting Pool** forms with the Washington Monument a gigantic sundial.*

KOREAN WAR VETERANS MEMORIAL

Documentary realism marks the Korean War Veterans Memorial. Making their way up a slope toward an American flag are 19 soldiers whose service affiliations, race and ethnicity, ages, uniforms, and equipment all represent the historical facts of America's involvement in the Korean War. The soldiers are reflected in a mural wall of polished black granite, etched with hundreds of faces of support personnel—engineers, medics, chaplains, suppliers of matériel—taken from more than 2,500 photographs preserved in the Department of Defense.

VIETNAM VETERANS MEMORIAL

Flowers, letters, photographs, and personal mementos left behind by visitors give the Vietnam Veterans Memorial an emotional immediacy that is unique in a city full of monuments and memorials. It is the most visited monument on the Mall. It is also the most controversial, just as the war it remembers. When the design competition was won by Maya Ying Lin, a Chinese-American student at Yale University, critics were appalled. Expecting something heroic in white marble, they were confronted instead with a V-shaped black slash in the earth. Where critics found defeatist gloom Lin envisoned regeneration. "Take a knife and cut open the earth," she is quoted as saying, "and with time the grass will heal it." A walk along "the wall" takes the visitor into the dark earth, past the 50,000 etched names of every single American killed in the war, and out again into the light and air.

The soldiers of the Korean War Veterans Memorial (above) are sculpted by **Frank C. Gaylord II**.
The **polished black marble wall** *of the Vietnam Memorial (left and below) contains the names of the 50,000 Americans killed in the war.*

Anchoring the western end of the Mall, the Lincoln Memorial stands as a **temple to American ideals.**

The **seated statue of Lincoln** conveys a sense of both power and gentleness.

LINCOLN MEMORIAL

One of the most familiar icons in American culture (it figures on the back of the five-dollar bill), the Lincoln Memorial performs a series of symbolic functions. It anchors the Mall on its western end, counterbalancing the Capitol at the eastern end. At the same time it commemorates the president whose fate it was to save the union. In doing so, it gives inescapable physical presence to the man and to his words. Daniel Chester French's statue of the seated Lincoln, modeled over a period of thirteen years, is constructed out of twenty separate blocks of Georgia marble, but so skillfully joined together that they give the impression of a single mass. The spirit communicated by that 19-foot-high mass is, however, touchingly human.

Ornament in a monumental landscape, memorial to a slain president, translation of words and deeds into stone, the Lincoln Memorial also functions as a symbol of civil rights struggles in America. Standing atop reclaimed marshland, the building itself puts the shape and structural elements of a Greek Doric temple to decidedly modern uses. Henry Bacon, the architect, has given access, unusually, from one of temple's broad sides. The 36 columns represent the states of the union at the time of Lincoln's death.

Standing amid cherry trees in Potomac Park, along one side of the **Tidal Basin,** the Jefferson Memorial forms one of the most famous icons of Washington.

Ionic columns (left) encircle Rudolph Evans's **bronze statue of President Jefferson.**

JEFFERSON MEMORIAL

If Thomas Jefferson had won the design competition for the president's house (instead of James Hoban), visitors to the Jefferson Memorial would be able to stand on the steps of this miniature, open-air Pantheon, look across the Tidal Basin, and see in the distance a version of Palladio's domed Villa Rotunda closing the prospect. The vista between the Jefferson Memorial and the White House forms a north-south axis that crosses the east-west axis of the Mall near the Washington Monument. Incumbents in the White House, at least since the Jefferson Memorial was completed in 1943, have looked out the window at a constant reminder of America's polymath third president. Jefferson would have approved of the view. His own design for the new capital featured public walks connecting the major buildings. Fittingly, it was Jefferson's own architectural designs (for the president's house, for the Rotunda Building at the University of Virginia, for his private retreat Monticello) that inspired John Russell Pope's design for the Jefferson Memorial. Rudolph Evans's bronze statue of the president stands amid encircling Ionic columns and four panels with stirring excerpts from Jefferson's speeches and writings. Views of the Jefferson Memorial nestled amid the blossoming cherry trees of the Tidal Basin have emerged as the travel-poster image of Washington, D.C. It is all the more ironic that the spectacle can be enjoyed for only a week to ten days each year (in late March or early April) and that the trees have been the subject of repeated political controversy. The Tidal Basin, having started out as a strictly utilitarian device for flushing the nearby Washington Channel with fresh river water, first acquired its Yoshino cherry trees, a gift from Japan, in 1912, but only after diplomatic embarrassment when the first shipment of trees had to be burned because they were infested with insect pests and fungus diseases. After the Japanese attack on Pearl Harbor in 1941, vandals destroyed several of the trees. When trees were being removed to make way for the Jefferson Memorial, angry protestors plopped themselves down into the holes that were left and chained themselves to the survivors. A happier political event was the shipping of cuttings to Japan in 1952 to replace some of the parent trees.

The Jefferson Memorial incorporates **Roman architectural elements**— *in particular the circular design of the Pantheon—that Jefferson favored in his own building plans.*

The **bronze statue of President Jefferson** *(right), wearing a greatcoat supposed to have been given to him by the Polish patriot Thadeus Kosciuszko.*

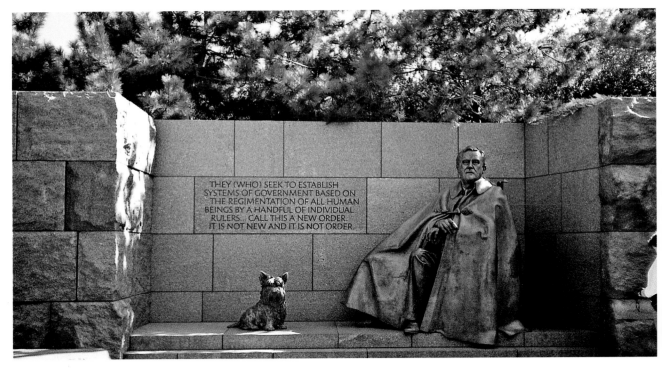

THEY (WHO) SEEK TO ESTABLISH
SYSTEMS OF GOVERNMENT BASED ON
THE REGIMENTATION OF ALL HUMAN
BEINGS BY A HANDFUL OF INDIVIDUAL
RULERS... CALL THIS A NEW ORDER.
IT IS NOT NEW AND IT IS NOT ORDER.

*In the **third room** of the Memorial, president Roosevelt appears as a seated figure; his beloved dog Fala sits nearby.*

FRANKLIN DELANO ROOSEVELT MEMORIAL

Franklin Delano Roosevelt (FDR) Memorial is along the famous Cherry Tree Walk on the Tidal Basin near the National Mall. The site for the FDR Memorial is located on an axis of the 1901 McMillan Plan which also includes the locations of the nation's Presidential monuments and memorials to Washington, Jefferson and Lincoln. Encompassing over seven acres, the FDR Memorial provides a historical narrative of President Roosevelt's twelve years in office from 1933 to 1945 in a park-like setting of four outdoor gallery rooms, one for each of FDR's terms in office. San Francisco architect Lawrence Halprin has created an emotionally compelling design, of natural landscaping, water, sculpture and quotations carved in walls of carnelian granite.

Visitors to the memorial enter the series of gallery rooms by first passing through the **Eagle Alcove,** which contains this inscription: "This generation of Americans has a rendezvous with destiny."

Room One sets the stage for FDR's presidency with Tom Hardy's large bas-relief bronze sculpture of the Great Seal of the President as it appeared at President Roosevelt's first inauguration. Next, a life-sized bas-relief depicts FDR waving from an open car during the parade of his first inaugural.

As visitors stroll to **Room Two**, images of the Great Depression appear. Three sculptural ensembles

by George Segal capture the mood of the times: DESPAIR – A worn and weary rural couple; HUNGER – Life-sized figures in a breadline; and HOPE – An intent figure of a man listening to one of FDR's famous "fireside chats" on a radio. Roosevelt's New Deal legislation is commemorated in a wall-sized bas-relief sculpture which faces five free-standing columns by artist Robert Graham.

A grassy berm between the second and third rooms marks the historical point at which Roosevelt and the nation confronted World War II.

In **Room Three**, the granite wall which has guided visitors through the Memorial is reduced to rubble, symbolizing the havoc of war. The room is dominated by a 9-foot-tall sculpture by Neil Estern of FDR, seated, his cape draped around him and his dog Fala at his feet.

In **Room Four**, the theme becomes The Seeds of Peace as Roosevelt enters his last term in office at the end of World War II. A dramatic waterfall cascades to a series of sparkling pools, creating a water garden on the edge of a dramatic plaza. Eleanor Roosevelt is depicted in a sculpture by Neil Estern with the United Nations symbol in the background – the first time a First Lady has been so honored. A 30-foot-long bas-relief by Leonard Baskin depicts Roosevelt's funeral cortege – his bier on a caisson pulled by horses with mourners following.

WORLD WAR II MEMORIAL

The National World War II Memorial is the nation's first monument dedicated to the conflict that left such a major imprint on the United States and the entire world. The memorial celebrates America's unit and power during World War II: 16 million servicemen and women, over 400,000 dead and continuous, dedicated support from the millions who helped their country at home.

Many visitors realize its meaning and impact merely by passing through the memorial. In fact, the memorial designed by Friedrich St. Florian, the architect who won the nationwide competition, welcomes visitors into an atmosphere of quiet, a feeling of community and participation in that historic endeavor. The memorial, that was unveiled by President George W. Bush in 2004, comprises a central plaza with fountains and waterfalls; it is encircled by 56 pillars (each one stands 17 feet high) representing the 48 states at the time of the war, Hawaii, Alaska, the District of Columbia, the Virgin Islands, Puerto Rico, Guam, the Commonwealth of the Philippines and American Samoa.

Inside the memorial are granite and bronze sculptures and 24 panels depicting the crucial phases of the war. The 4,000 gold stars one for each hundred, proudly commemorate the 400,000 who gave their lives in the defense of freedom. And finally, two majestic pavilions, Atlantic and Pacific, represent the main theaters of the war. The memorial was commissioned by the American Battle Monuments Commission and is now managed by the National Park Service, which sanctioned its listing among the United States national parks.

*The National World War II Memorial stands on the **National Mall** between the Washington Monument and the Lincoln Memorial.*

THE WHITE HOUSE

Television news broadcasts have made The White House one of the most recognized images in the world. Having first seen it close up on a television screen, many first-time visitors are struck by the modest size of what is, after all, an eighteenth-century country house enveloped by a huge city. The surroundings were altogether different when Abigail Adams moved in with her husband John, the second president, in 1800. "The country round is romantic," she wrote to her sister, "but a wild wilderness at present." Under construction since 1792, the building still was not finished when the Adamses arrived, and Mrs. Adams used the East Room for hanging out the laundry. Jefferson, the next occupant, found the place "big enough for two emperors, one Pope, and the grand Lama." His own design for the building, submitted anonymously, had been passed over in favor of one by James Hoban, an Irish-American who was a self-taught architect. To offset the pompous effect, Jefferson added two low-lying terrace-pavilions that are still used for offices and service functions. Succeeding occupants have left their own marks on the place, notably Harry Truman, who upset purists by adding a balcony to the curved South Portico, and Jacqueline Kennedy, who cleared out a century and a half of accumulated furnishings and restored the public rooms to something like their early nineteenth-century appearance. The most disastrous moment in White

The south portico of the White House incorporates a homey balcony added by President Harry Truman. The south lawn is the scene of parties and receptions, as well as the president's arrivals and departures by helicopter.

39

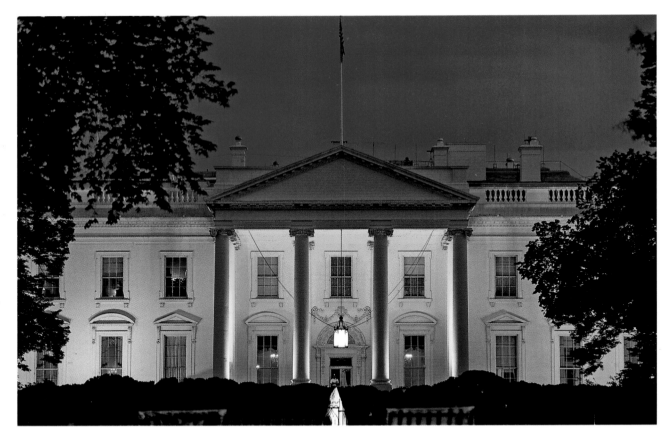

The **north portico** (above) forms the ceremonial entrance to the White House.

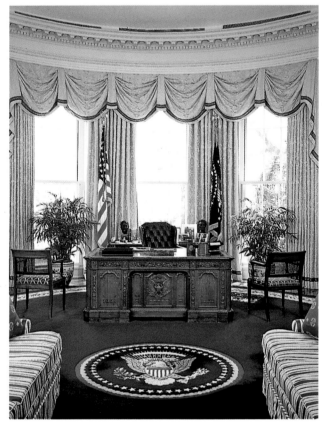

The **Oval Office,** situated in an extension of one of the terraces added by Jefferson, has been the workplace of every president since William Howard Taft in 1909.

House history came in August 1814, when the British invaded Washington and set the building afire. Dolly Madison, left alone to hold the house, managed to get out just in time, first sending away "the plate and most valuable portable articles belonging to the house," as well as Gilbert Stuart's full-length portrait of George Washington, which still dominates the East Room. A violent summer thunderstorm saved the house from total destruction. Hoban's reconstruction of the building over the next four years included a coat of white wash, perhaps to hide scorch marks from the British flames. The name "White House," in use from the very beginning to describe the structure's creamy sandstone, did not become official until 1902.

LAFAYETTE SQUARE

Lafayette Square became a square when Thomas Jefferson, objecting to imperial pretense, detached it from the grounds of the White House. It became Lafayette Square in 1824 when the Revolutionary War hero was feted there. By the mid-nineteenth century it had become a fashionable address, as witness the elegant townhouses that surround it on three sides. Andrew Jackson, hero of the Battle of New Orleans (1814), rides proud in the center.

BLAIR HOUSE

Two once separate houses have been joined together to form guest quarters for visiting dignitaries and heads-of-state. The original Blair House, built in 1824, acquired its name when it was purchased in 1837 by Francis P. Blair, friend of Andrew Jackson and founder of the pro-Jackson *Washington Globe*. The house next door was built in 1859 by Admiral Phillips Lee as a gift to his bride Elizabeth, daughter of Francis Blair. While the White House was being renovated during the 1950s Blair House provided temporary quarters for President Harry Truman and his family.

Clark Mills's **statue of Andrew Jackson** *(right), erected in 1853, was the first equestrian statue to be designed and cast by an American. A 15-foot gilt statue of Winged Victory crowns the World War I* **First Division Memorial***, south of the Old Executive Office Building (below).*

CONSTITUTION HALL

V iolinist Efrem Zimbalist inaugurated what for many years was Washington's only major concert hall. With a capacity of 4000, it remains Washington's largest. John Russell Pope's edifice, built to house conventions of the Daughters of the American Revolution, was completed in 1929.

ORGANIZATION OF AMERICAN STATES

T he world's oldest international organization—a federation of the nations of North, South, and Central America established in 1890—is housed in a white marble building that brings together stylistic elements of many cultures. Within a Beaux Arts frame are to be found a tropical patio built around a fountain that combines Mayan, Aztec, and Zapotecan motifs, Aztec gardens, and a gallery devoted to contemporary art.

*James Earle Fraser's statue of **Alexander Hamilton,** first Secretary of the Treasury (1789-95), presides over the south entrance plaza to the Treasury Building.*

*The classical facade of the **Constitution Hall,** (opposite page,above) along 17th Street, N.W., composes one of Washington's noblest vistas. The **Organization of American States** (opposite page, below) occupies a building that, like the organization itself, combines several distinct cultures.*

TREASURY BUILDING

Andrew Jackson is supposed to have said "*Here* is where I want the cornerstone," and *there* the Treasury Building is—blocking L'Enfant's planned vista between the White House and Capitol. Jackson was impatient with political squabbling about where the new building should be. Both of its predecessors had burned. Jackson walked out of the White House one morning (so the story goes), planted his cane in the ground, made his declaration, and that was that. The vista may be gone, but the stately Greek Revival building that arose in its place is one of Washington's best known landmarks. (It figures on the back of the ten-dollar bill.) Robert Mills contributed the original design and survived political skirmishes long enough to complete the middle portion of the east range. The rest of the project was carried out between 1836 and 1869 by a succession of other architects. Recent restoration to the interior has returned spaces like the two-story Cash Room to their original splendor.

FBI

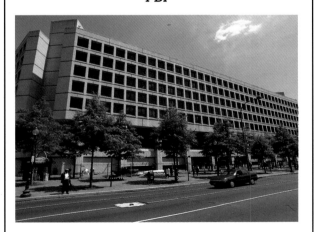

No secrecy here. The headquarters of the Federal Bureau of Investigation asserts its presence in a huge fortress-like building erected amid great public controversy in 1974. Designed by Stanley Gladych in the idiom of Le Corbusier's "International Style," the structure plays on a contrast between heavy concrete building material and airy weightlessness. Blocks of offices are suspended between tower-like pylons.

OLD POST OFFICE BUILDING

Neoclassical conformists hate it; admirers of the odd and the eccentric love it. Amid the Roman regularities of the Federal Triangle, the Old Post Office Building (1899) refuses to be awed. Its clock tower (with hands 5.5 and 7.5 feet long) rises high above its neighbors and insinuates itself into the view anywhere a stroller happens to be along Pennsylvania Avenue. Office workers and school groups throng the atrium's food court and sight-seers ride the open-cage elevator to the clock tower, while officials of the National Endowments for the Arts and the Humanities work away in upstairs offices.

MARKET SQUARE

Now the site of two *neo*-neoclassical buildings erected in 1990, Market Square was indeed a vegetable and meat market until the City Beautiful movement banished such functions to less prominent locations during the first decade of the twentieth century. Earlier visitors describe a lively scene at this location, as boarding-house keepers thronged the stalls to do their daily shopping. Today's visitors will find a pair of monumental colonnades embracing a semicircular space in which a brace of masts and a lone bronze figure keep watch as the Navy Memorial. The Market Square development, which houses shops, offices, restaurants, and condominiums, fits in well with its neoclassical neighbors across Pennsylvania Avenue at the same time that it contributes to the liveliness of the nearby Seventh Street art and theater district.

*Inside and out, the idiosyncratic **Old Post Office Building** (above) offers welcome relief from the neo-classical regularities of official Washington.*

*The **Navy Memorial** (left) occupies an open space along Pennsylvania Avenue that was once a bustling produce market.*

LINCOLN'S ASSASSINATION

The date was April 14, 1865. The Civil War had ended five days before, when Robert E. Lee had surrendered to Ulysses S. Grant at Appomattox, Virginia. At John T. Ford's two-year-old theater on Tenth Street Tom Taylor's comedy *Our American Cousin* was slated for its final night, with the celebrated actress Laura Keene in one of the main roles. President Lincoln, an admirer of Miss Keene, was advertised

*Ford's Theater, the **scene of President Lincoln's assassination** in 1865, has been restored as both a memorial and a working theater.*

on playbills as planning to attend. Also in attendance that night was John Wilkes Booth, an actor whose performances Lincoln had twice enjoyed at Ford's Theater. Near the beginning of the second act Booth, who was well known to the theater management, gained access to the president's box and, taking advantage of the audience's laughter at a funny line, fired a shot point-blank into Lincoln's skull. He leapt to the stage to announce his vengence on behalf of the Confederacy and escaped into the night.

In a small back bedroom of a brick row house, the Petersen House, Lincoln died early in the morning of April 15. Doctors advised against taking the unconscious president back to the White House over rough cobbled streets.

The little house had been built in 1849 by William Petersen, a Swedish immigrant who worked as a tailor on the first floor and rented out rooms to lodgers. The back bedroom belonged to his daughter Pauline, who was away at boarding school. When restoration began on the house in the 1920s Pauline Petersen Wenzing was able to give precise information about the room's furnishings. Visitors to the site today can see the parlor in which Mrs.

Lincoln waited, the room in which the secretary of war carried out his investigation of the crime, and the bedroom in which Lincoln died.

The bed itself is a reproduction, but on it lies one of the bloodied pillows that cushioned the president's head.

*Period furnishings, including pieces original to the house, make the **Petersen House** feel much as it did on April 15, 1865, when the wounded Lincoln died in a **small back bedroom** (left).*

The **National Portrait Gallery** and the **Museum of American Art** occupy premises that have served as the capital's first art museum, a conservatory for exotic plants, a Civil War hospital, a museum of patented inventions, and the site of presidential balls.

DOWNTOWN

NATIONAL PORTRAIT GALLERY

A monument to Greek sobriety in a city of Roman excess, the complex of buildings that house the National Portrait Gallery and the Museum of American Art occupies a site that L'Enfant reserved for a "shrine to American heroes." The Portrait Gallery serves that function today, but only after the buildings housed the Patent Office, a Civil War hospital, and the Civil Service Commission. Begun in 1836 according to the solid, fire-proof designs of Robert Mills, the buildings were the largest in the entire country when they were completed in 1867— the nineteenth-century equivalent of the Pentagon. The colonnaded Lincoln Gallery encapsulates the buildings' history. Walt Whitman saw the gallery decked out for Lincoln's second inaugural ball in 1865, just months after he had helped Clara Barton, founder of the Red Cross, tend mortally wounded soldiers in the same room. Today the gallery houses modernist paintings from the collection of the Museum of American Art, which started out as the National Institute, in this very building, in 1841.

NATIONAL BUILDING MUSEUM

The National Building Museum stands as testimony to how one era's white elephant can become another era's architectural treasure. Having helped to engineer the Capitol's new dome during the Civil War, Montgomery C. Meigs, quartermaster general of the Union Army, was asked after the war to design a building for distributing military pensions. This gargantuan red-brick version of Michelangelo's Palazzo Farnese was the result. Inside is to be found one of Washington's truly stupendous spaces, a colonnaded atrium 316 feet long, 116 feet wide, and 159 feet high. A huge clerestory admits enough light to keep the interior bright in winter and enough air to keep it cool in summer. The Corinthian columns carrying the roof, 15 feet taller than the colossal columns at Baalbek, may be the largest Roman columns ever constructed. Recently restored after a century of critical abuse and physical neglect, the structure now houses the National Building Museum, dedicated to an appreciation of all kinds of buildings, in all kinds of circumstances.

PHILLIPS COLLECTION

The first gallery of modern art in America still feels like a private home. Small rooms invite intimate viewing. Sofas and chairs provide places to sit down. Sunday afternoon concerts in the music room send music drifting all over the house. The Phillips Collection, opened to the public in 1921, was indeed the private home of the collectors, Duncan and Marjorie Phillips—though not for long. Their generosity soon forced them to move to new quarters. The house itself had been built by Duncan Phillips's father in 1897. The personal taste of the collectors distinguishes the paintings on view. Giorgione, El Greco, Goya, Daumier, Thomas Eakins, and Winslow Homer share space with the artists for which the collection is noted: Van Gogh, Monet, Bonnard, Gauguin, Klee, Braque, Picasso, Mark Rothko, and Georgia O'Keefe. Most famous of all, perhaps, is Renoir's "The Boating Party." The public to whom the Phillipses introduced these modern artists included future members of the Washington Colorist School.

THE BUREAU OF ENGRAVING AND PRINTING

The Bureau of Engraving and Printing, an agency of the United States Department of the Treasury is headquartered here in Washington D.C. It is here that the financial and other securities of the United States are manufactured. The Bureau designs and prints Federal Reserve notes as well as White House invitations, Treasury securities, identification cards and other government documents that require special security.
Banknotes are produced at the Bureau and at its facility in Fort Worth, Texas, while all coins are produced by the United States Mint.
For over a century, until 2005 the Bureau also issued stamps for the U. S. Postal Service. Today, one of the Bureau's main activities is research and development In the fields of automation in the production process and counterfeit deterrent technologies for use in security documents and mainly the U.S. currency it produces. There is a seventy year program in place for the design and manufacture of our paper money to guarantee absolute protection of its authenticity.

*The monumental exterior (above) of the **National Building Museum**. Distant memories of ancient Rome and Michelangelo haunt the interior (middle) of the building.*

*Since it was established in 1861, the **Bureau of Engraving** (right) has been printing many important federal documents and in 1877 became the sole printer of U.S. currency. Even today, it is the largest producer of security documents for the entire nation.*

Civil War General **Philip H. Sheridan** holds down one of Embassy Row's strategic positions.

The **Basilica of the National Shrine of the Immaculate Conception** is a National Historic Landmark.

EMBASSY ROW

Partly a legacy of Gilded Age extravagence, partly a showcase of modern and post-modern design, Embassy Row stretches along Massachusetts Avenue, N.W., from Dupont Circle to Washington National Cathedral. Many of the buildings that today house foreign legations, especially toward the Dupont Circle end, were built as private residences between 1880 and 1910. Their owners were tycoons who had made their money elsewhere but were taking up residence in Washington to give their wealth an aura of gentility and to gain handy access to the corridors of power. Mansions that looked like French châteaux, Palladian palazzi, and Mayfair townhouses served their purposes nicely.

NATIONAL SHRINE

This is the eight largest Catholic church in the world and the biggest in the nation.
When the American diocese requested that it be built in 1846 the aim was to erect a building that would be original and peculiar to the United States as testimony of devotion to the nation's patron saint, the Virgin Mary. These intentions are fully reflected in the style and symbolism of its architecture. The Byzantine interior has a seven-foot high statue of Mary Immaculate, a bronze dove symbolizing the Holy Spirit and many items of artistic interest that include a twentieth century series of mosaics. The exterior of the church is essential Romanesque in stile, symbolizing a return to the purity and joy of Medieval Catholicism.
The result is a truly original church, one that is not modeled on or a copy of any other, but the fruit of the devotion of American Catholics.

*Commanding a prospect over the city from Mount St. Alban, **Washington National Cathedral** was under construction for most of the twentieth century.*

*Every detail of the cathedral's **interior** was carried out by craftsmen using medieval techniques.*

WASHINGTON NATIONAL CATHEDRAL

L'Enfant's vision of a "great church for national purpose ... equally open to all" has been realized only in the twentieth century with the construction of the Washington National Cathedral. Begun in 1907, the building was finished in 1990. Although erected under auspices of the Protestant Episcopal Church, the cathedral defines its mission as ecumenical. Funerals and memorial services for many national heroes have been held there. Chapels within the cathedral have provided parish homes for Polish, Russo-Carpathian, Syrian, and Serbian Orthodox churches. Martin Luther King, Jr., preached his last Sunday sermon from the cathedral's pulpit. Only a single vote prevented the cathedral from being built in the neoclassical style of most of Washington's public buildings. Constructed in the idiom of fourteenth-century English Gothic, using medieval building techniques, Washington National Cathedral may well be the last great Gothic building to be attempted anywhere in the world.

*This aerial view shows how Georgetown, even today, remains a **self-contained town** within the city of Washington.*

*Lined with warehouses and factories that have been converted to stylish uses, the **Chesapeake and Ohio Canal** (below) was once Georgetown's link to the wild west.*

GEORGETOWN

C&O CANAL

Retaining today its own social identity and architectural distinction, Georgetown was an established community within the state of Maryland two generations before the District of Columbia and the City of Washington were ever envisioned. It was at a gathering in Mayor Uriah Forrest's townhouse, still standing at 3350 M Street, N.W., that local landowners were persuaded by George Washington to sell to the federal government the tracts needed for laying out the new capital to the east of town. The "George" in Georgetown was not George Washington but King George II (reigned 1727-1760), father of the king who received the Declaration of Independence. As settlers pressed westward into Virginia, Maryland, and the frontier beyond, Georgetown stood to expand its shipping trade—but for one obstacle: the Great Falls of the Potomac just upriver. At the close of the Revolutionary War, George Washington was one of several investors in a project to build a canal detour around the falls. Substantial remains of the canal still can be seen in Great Falls Park, Virginia. In 1828 a more ambitious project was begun, to build a canal all the way from Georgetown to Ohio. By the time the first 185 miles had been completed, the railroad had already beat the Chesapeake and Ohio Canal to its western markets. Georgetown then settled into genteel obsolesence while the brash new federal city all around it grew by leaps and bounds. In 1871 Georgetown lost its charter and self-government, officially becoming part of the City of Washington for the first time.

Warehouses and mills along the C&O canal have recently been converted into offices, shops, art galleries, restaurants, and condominiums.

OLD STONE HOUSE

Washington's oldest surviving building, the Old Stone House in Georgetown was built about 1766 by Christopher Layman, who lived in the house and ran a cabinet-making shop there. At the time, Georgetown had been established for only fifteen years or so. Major land grants in the area date to 1703, when Ninian Beall obtained a patent for The Rock of Dumbarton. George Gordon soon established Rock Creek Plantation nearby. Other settlers, many of them Scots like Beall and Gordon, arrived over the next forty years. Export of tobacco from up-country plantations and import of household goods and rum provided the reason for the port city's establishment in 1751. At the time Georgetown stood on the western frontier of colonial civilization. The humble proportions and rough-hewn functionality of the Old Stone House help explain why Abigail Adams, moving into the still unfinished White House in 1800, could exclaim, "Such a place as Georgetown! … It is the very dirtyest Hole I ever saw for a place of any trade or respectability of inhabitants." The great federal houses that distinguish Georgetown today were, in 1766, still more than thirty years in the future.

*Simple in design and sturdy in construction, the Old Stone House (above) is **Washington's oldest surviving building.** The interior (below) is as spare as the exterior.*

FEDERAL HOUSES

The 3300 block of N Street, N.W., (formerly First Street) typifies the federal architecture that abounds in Georgetown. Geometrical simplicity and plainness of detail distinguish the federal houses of Georgetown from their more ornamented Georgian counterparts in Old Town Alexandria down the river. "Cox's Row," as the 3300 block is called, was built between 1815 and 1818 by John Cox, a merchant who served as mayor of Georgetown for 22 years. When in 1824-25 the Marquis de Lafayette payed his last visit to the country he had helped to liberate, Cox offered the house that is now number 3337 as a temporary residence. Lafayette accepted the offer. In social scale the townhouses of Cox's Row were midway between great estates like Dumbarton House and the humbler houses of workers and artisans. Until the 1960s Georgetown was home to an economically diverse population, including a substantial African-American community. Mount Zion United Methodist Church, thought to be the oldest African-American congregation in Washington, traces its history back to 1816 and still holds services in a late nineteenth-century building at 1334 29th Street, N.W., on Georgetown's eastern side.

DUMBARTON HOUSE

Dating to about 1798, Dumbarton House is probably the oldest of the great houses that crown the heights above Georgetown.
The others are Evermay (1801), Dumbarton Oaks (1801), the Bowie-Sevier House (1805), and Tudor Place (1816).
Dumbarton, like most of the others, was originally connected with a great tract of land.
The first owner of the site was Ninian Beall, who in 1703 secured a patent for 705 acres which he called "The Rock of Dumbarton," after the castle along the River Clyde in his Scottish homeland. The tract included much of the land on which Georgetown stands today. The extant house was designed and built by its first owner, Samuel Johnson. When Joseph Nourse, holder of important positions under Washington, Jefferson, and Madison, acquired the property about 1805, he ordered important alterations to be carried out by Benjamin Henry Latrobe, one of the architects of the original U. S. Capitol.
Dumbarton House serves today as headquarters of the National Society of the Colonial Dames of America.

*The dominant feel of Georgetown comes from houses constructed in the early years of the federal republic, like **"Cox's Row"** along what once was called First Street.*

*Eighteenth- and early nineteenth-century mansions line the heights above Georgetown. **Dumbarton House** is the oldest.*

GEORGETOWN PARK

The feed stores, automobile repair shops, pharmacies, and hardware stores that once served Georgetown as a working community have given way for the most part to art galleries, antique stores, bars, restaurants, coffee houses, clothing boutiques, upscale food markets, and bookstores. A relic of the old days survives in Stohlman's Confectionary Shop (founded 1854), the interior of which was removed in 1957 from a building still standing at 1254 Wisconsin Avenue and is now reconstructed inside the Museum of American History on the Mall. Examples of the new wave of shops are concentrated in Georgetown Park, a 1980s development that incorporates several older buildings into a sprawling, multi-storied shopping mall

*Commerce has always been the reason for Georgetown's existence. The enclosed spaces of **Georgetown Park** (above) have joined **small shops in older structures** to ensure Georgetown's contemporary reputation as a stylish shopping destination.*

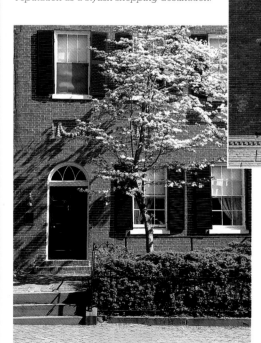

*A **trompe-l'oeil** evocation of eighteenth-century Georgetown (above) joins **the real thing** (left) to give the neighborhood its antique charm.*

with skylights, tile floors, and cast-iron fittings that recall the shopping galleries of nineteenth-century European cities. Among the historic structures that adjoin Georgetown Park are an early nineteenth-century firehouse and one of Washington's original public food markets.

KEY BRIDGE

The magnificent arches of Key Bridge have spanned the Potomac River at one of its most scenic reaches since 1923. The bridge takes its name from Francis Scott Key's mansion, which stood nearby. It was from this house that Key departed by boat on September 12, 1814, and made his way by water to Baltimore, to rescue a friend who had been captured by the British. While anchored in Baltimore harbor, Key witnessed the British bombardment of the city and was inspired to write "The Star-Spangled Banner."

GEORGETOWN UNIVERSITY

History, academic reputation, a renowned basketball team, famous alumni, and a scenic campus draw visitors to the gates of Georgetown University. The oldest Catholic institution of higher learning in the United States, the university traces its history to an academy founded in 1789. The towered Healy Building (1879), named for Patrick Healy, a partly African-American Jesuit priest who served as president of the university in the nineteenth century, dominates the campus and the view from the Potomac. Behind the granite facade are to be found federalist red-brick reminders of the university's more distant past, particularly Old North Hall (1792-93), from the steps of which George Washington addressed the student body.

KENNEDY CENTER AND WATERGATE

Vast public spaces, six performance venues, and a performing arts library make up a living memorial to John F. Kennedy. Although a cultural center for the nation's capital had been discussed since the 1930s, it took the assassination of an arts-minded president to get one built. Edward Durrell Stone's modernist restatement of the Lincoln Memorial, situated just down the river, opened in 1971. The grand foyer, 630 feet long and six stories high, is dominated by a huge bust of Kennedy by Robert Berks. Unlike many real-estate ventures in America, the Italian-designed Watergate Complex is named for a real place. Just down the river, where Arlington Memorial Bridge crosses Rock Creek Parkway, a huge arc of steps leads down from the Lincoln Memorial to the shores of the Potomac. This original Watergate, built in 1931, was designed to receive important visitors who might arrive by water. The steps' 1971 namesake is one of Washington's most prestigious addresses as well as the site of political espionage that cost Richard Nixon his job as president.

*Georgetown's historic connection to the Potomac River is affirmed by **Key Bridge** (below) and the **Washington Harbour** **development** (opposite page, above).*

*The **Watergate Complex** and the **Kennedy Center** (opposite page, below) front the Potomac River in Foggy Bottom.*

55

*The nine arches of **Memorial Bridge** (above) link the Mall with Arlington National Cemetery in Virginia. **Statues of the Arts of War and the Arts of Peace** (below) flank the Washington end of the bridge.*

*The **Tomb of the Unknown Soldier** (opposite page) is the most prominent among more than 200,000 graves that fill Arlington Cemetery's 420 acres.*

ARLINGTON

ARLINGTON MEMORIAL BRIDGE

According to Charles Moore, secretary to the McMillan Commission, it was a vista in the gardens of the Villa Borghese in Rome that inspired the commissioners to envision a low monumental bridge connecting the Lincoln Memorial with Arlington National Cemetery. It was a colossal traffic jam that got the bridge built. On Armistice Day 1921 a ceremonial motorcade bound for Arlington Cemetery got stuck for two hours trying to cross the Fourteenth Street Bridge and negotiate back roads from the bridge to the cemetery. Funding for the long-foreseen Memorial Bridge was soon forthcoming. The elegant nine-arched span was completed in 1932. Heroic statues of The Arts of War, by Leo Friedlander, and The Arts of Peace, by James Earle Fraser, anchor the Washington end of the bridge.

ARLINGTON NATIONAL CEMETERY

The Doric portico of Arlington House (built 1803-1818), a plantation house associated with the families of both George Washington and Robert E. Lee, commands two unrivaled views: one over the City of Washington and another over two centuries of American history in the form of 200,000 graves that fill Arlington National Cemetery. Slave labor built the mansion and worked the estate that was inhabited by George Washington Parke Custis, adopted son of George Washington. Robert E. Lee took possession of the plantation when he married Custis's only surviving child, Mary Ann Randolph Custis, in 1831. Today the cemetery covers 420 acres. Separate monuments to honor the dead of America's wars are centered on the Tomb of the Unknown Soldier, erected in 1931 to commemorate a soldier killed in World War I. Flat stones designate unknowns from more recent wars.

JOHN FITZGERALD KENNEDY GRAVESITE

Perhaps the most visited site in Arlington Cemetery is the grave of president John F. Kennedy, marked not with a marble monument but with some of the slain president's favorite plants, a view over the city, and a constantly burning flame.

Other members of the Kennedy family are buried nearby. The most recent addition to the grave site of JFK is the grave of his wife, Jacqueline Bouvier Kennedy Onassis.

MARINE CORPS WAR MEMORIAL

D uring the battle for the small Pacific island of Iwo Jima in February 1945 a small detachment of Marines climbed to the island's highest point and planted the American flag. Associated Press photographer Joe Rosenthal, a native Washingtonian, happened to be on hand and arranged for the soldiers to recreate the event for his camera. Instantly famous, the photograph won a Pulitzer Prize later that year. The image inspired Felix W. de Weldon to begin a sculpture of the heroic event. Cast in bronze six times life size, the 78-foot-high sculpture was dedicated on November 10, 1954, on the 179th anniversary of the Marine Corps.

NETHERLANDS CARILLON

T he site of one of the best views over Washington is occupied by a handsome modernist bell tower given by the people of the Netherlands in gratitude for American aid during and after the second World War. The ring of 49 bells was presented by Queen Juliana in 1952; the steel tower, 127 feet high, was dedicated in 1960. Dutch painter Piet Mondrian's abstract squares and lines seem to be the inspiration for the tower's design. Warm-weather concerts send melodies across the tulips and into the vista beyond.

Dutch friendship with America sounds out in the bells of the **Netherlands Carillon.**

Popularly known as the **Iwo Jima Monument** *(below), the Marine Corps War Memorial commemorates a decisive moment in World War II.*

HAITI·1915-1934 ⋆ SANTO·DOMINGO·1916-1924 ⋆ WORLD·WAR·I·1917-1918·BELLEAU·WOOD·SOISSONS·ST·MIHIEL

*From **the Pentagon** America's military campaigns have been directed since World War II.*

THE PENTAGON

Built as a command center for America's worldwide military forces during World War II (only the Navy operated out of separate premises), the Pentagon Building remains the headquarters of the Department of Defense. By every statistical measure, this building-within-a-building beggars description: 921 feet on each of the outer building's five sides, 360 feet on each of the inner building's five sides, an outer circumference of 4,605 feet, 7,748 windows, 17.5 miles of corridors, 92 acres of usable office space, 150 stairways, 280 restrooms, 685 drinking fountains, 4,200 installed clocks, 85,000 light fixtures, and parking spaces for 9,500 cars. Authorized by an act of Congress in the middle of the war, in 1941, the building was erected in 1942. It cost $85,000,000. The working population in the building has ranged from 22,718 in 1946, just after the close of World War II, to 31,419 in 1952, during the Korean War. More than 20,000 people—the equivalent of the population of a small city—work there today. The structure's vastness has given rise to a host of legends about people who entered, got lost, and found their way out after days of wandering, among them a messenger boy who entered the building on Friday and emerged on Monday as a lieutenant colonel. The War Department's move from the Old Executive Office Building, via a number of temporary locations, was a move from the largest office building in the world in the nineteenth century to the largest office building in the world in the twentieth century.

*The historic core of one of America's most historic communities is located in Alexandria's **Market Square.***

ALEXANDRIA

MARKET SQUARE

Founded in 1748, three years before Georgetown, Alexandria was likewise a flourishing tobacco port long before the City of Washington was dreamed of. A youthful George Washington helped lay out the streets of the new town, which soon became the focus of commerce and social activity for the plantations round about, among them Mount Vernon. Market square was the center of it all. On the square's southeastern corner stands the Ramsey House (1749-51), the oldest structure in the city. In a room of the nearby Carlyle House (1752) General Edward Braddock and five royally appointed governors of the colonies met to plan one of major campaigns of the French and Indian War (1753-1763). Next door is the Bank of Alexandria, organized in 1792. At the square's northwestern edge stands Gadsby's Tavern (erected in two stages, 1752 and 1792), which served as George Washington's military headquarters in 1754, when he was lieutenant-colonel of the Virginia Militia, and as the site of his last review of the troops just before his death in 1799.

OLD HOUSES

As federal architecture is Georgetown's distinctive style, so Georgian is Alexandria's. The streets of Old Town are lined with exquisitely detailed townhouses, shops, inns, schools, and churches dating from the late eighteenth and early nineteenth centuries. "Gentry Row" in the 200-block of Prince Street boasts some particularly spectacular examples. One block away the more modest houses of "Captains' Row" tumble down a cobbled street to the Potomac River. Along the waterfront warehouses of the same early period have been converted into shops and restaurants. The Stabler-Leadbeater Apothecary Shop, with its distinctive bow windows, is a rare example of a commercial establishment that has survived virtually unchanged since 1792. There is even a fire-fighting company that traces its origins to 1774. Among several historic churches, the real treasure is Christ Episcopal Church, built between 1767 and 1773. Inside, congregants of today read the Creed and the Lord's Prayer from wall tablets that have never been repainted. The original box pews include those occupied by George Washington's family and Robert E. Lee's.

Houses from the eighteenth and early nineteenth centuries *make Alexandria a treasury of American architecture.*

MASONIC NATIONAL MEMORIAL

GEORGE WASHINGTON MASONIC NATIONAL MEMORIAL

Riding high atop a site that was once proposed for the U. S. Capitol, the Masonic National Memorial in Alexandria, Virginia, preserves priceless relics associated with George Washington within a building that was designed to recall one of the Seven Wonders of the Ancient World, the lighthouse at Alexandria, Egypt. Like many of the republic's early leaders,

George Washington was a Free Mason. He was first master of the Alexandria Lodge, chartered in 1788. Over the years the lodge acquired many pieces of Washington memorabilia, some of which were lost in 1871 when a fire destroyed the lodge's original quarters on Market Square. The remainder are preserved today in a replica of the eighteenth-century lodge room, located within the Masonic National Memorial. On display in the room are the high-back leather chair Washington used while grand master, a pen knife given to him by his mother, his pocket compass, the silver trowel he used to lay the cornerstone of the Capitol, a letter he wrote a few weeks before his death (declining an invitation to a ball), the bleeding instruments used on his deathbed, and the clock from his bedchamber at Mount Vernon, stopped forever at the moment of his death, 10:20 on the evening of December 14, 1799.

A pastel portrait of Washington by William Williams of Philadelphia shows the former president six years before his death. Unlike the more famous oil portraits, Williams' likeness of Washington shows an aged man, complete with small-pox scars, a wound on the left cheek, and a mole behind the right ear. Altogether different is the heroic statue of Washington that presides over the Masonic Memorial's grand entrance hall. The cornerstone to the edifice was laid in 1923, using the silver trowel Washington himself had used at the Capitol. Paid for by 3,200,000 Masons throughout the United States, the building was dedicated in 1932. The tower rises 400 feet above the town below and commands a magnificent panorama in all directions.

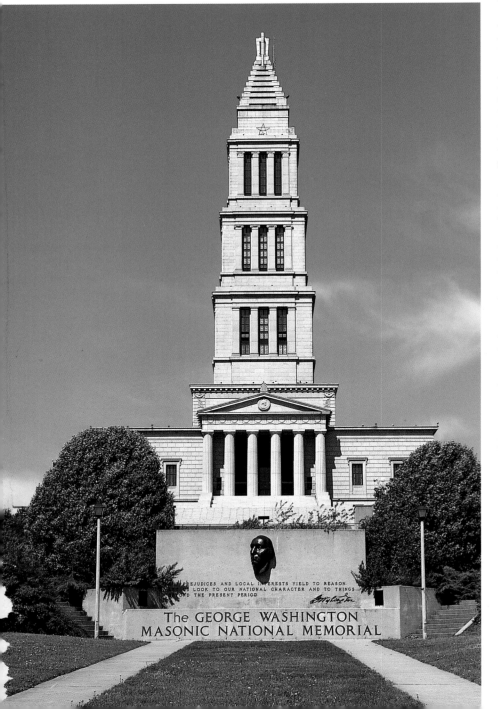

PREJUDICES AND LOCAL INTERESTS YIELD TO REASON.
LOOK TO OUR NATIONAL CHARACTER AND TO THINGS
BEYOND THE PRESENT PERIOD

The GEORGE WASHINGTON
MASONIC NATIONAL MEMORIAL

The **ancient lighthouse at Alexandria, Egypt,** provided the inspiration for the Masonic Memorial's design (left).

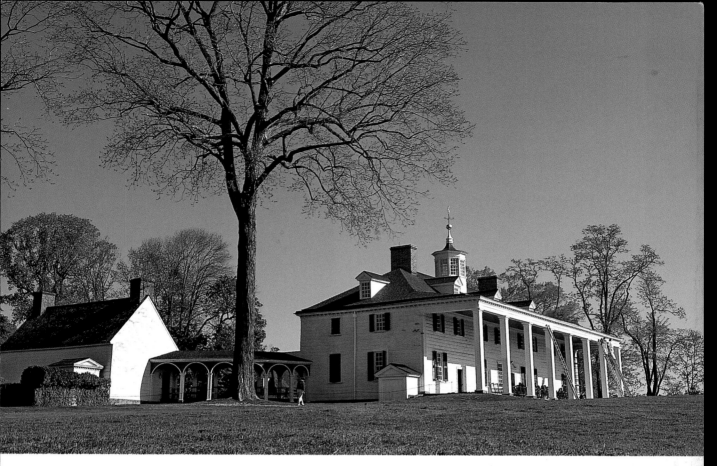

*Not only the **mansion house** (above) but outlying buildings and **artefacts of everyday life** (below) make Mount Vernon a museum of colonial America as well as a memorial to America's first president.*

MOUNT VERNON

A shrine to the commander in chief of the Revolutionary Army and first President of the United States, Mount Vernon gives visitors a good sense of the agricultural life that George Washington, like many of his peers, left behind when he went to war with Britain and assumed public office. Washington, for one, always longed to get back to the land. The family estate, originally encompassing 5000 acres, had been patented by his ancestor John Washington in 1674. It was George's elder brother Lawrence who started the house that stands today and named it for his old commander, Admiral Edward Vernon of the British navy. The "mount" came naturally enough: the house stands atop a bluff that commands a splendid view of the Potomac. The wide veranda and large cupola that form the house's most distinctive features were added during a major remodeling that George Washington began in 1773. The clapboard siding of the all-wood structure was coated with sand to give the impression of stone

Washington's tomb (above) and *eighteenth-century gardens* (right) offer opportunities for quiet reflection amid one of America's most visited destinations.

blocks. Arched breezeways connect the main house to service buildings that formed, in Washington's day, a self-sustaining country village. Here cotton, wool, and even silk were spun and woven; candles were molded; butter was churned; grapes were pressed and wine was casked; maize and wheat were milled. More than 200 slaves were required to farm the estate and keep it supplied and fed. In his will Washington instructed that the slaves should be freed upon the death of his wife. Near the house a flower garden, planted with eighteenth-century varieties, is laid out according to Washington's original plan. The interior of the main house retains some of the original furnishings. Particularly striking are the large and stylish Banquet Hall, with its Adam-inspired ceiling; the Family Dining Room, where Washington kept open house for a steady stream of visitors; the Library, with the desk and chair Washington used while directing the estate; and the upstairs bedroom containing the bed on which Washington died. In a shady recess down the hillside stands the national hero's simple tomb.